1

2

3

6

7

8

9

10

11

12

13

14

15

16

17

18

19

20

21

22

23

24

25

26

27

28

29

30

31

32

33

34

35

36

37

38

39

THANKSSGIVING

41

43

45

47

48

49

50

51

55

56

59

60

63

65

66

67

69

70

73

76

80

Discover the timeless joy of colouring with "Colorful Journeys: Exploring Worlds and Wonders," a colouring book that offers a serene escape to creativity and tranquillity for all ages.

Key Features:

- Creativity & Stress Relief: Escape to a world of imagination with this proven stress reliever, perfect for finding peace in today's fast-paced world.
- Educational & Cultural Enrichment: Each page is a learning journey featuring architectural marvels, natural wonders, and global cultures to spark curiosity.
- Ideal for All Ages: Whether for family bonding, personal relaxation, or improving fine motor skills and artistic precision, this book suits anyone from children to adults.
- Therapeutic Benefits: Known for its calming effects, colouring helps reduce anxiety and enhance focus.
- Unique Artistic Content: Enjoy unrivalled artistic journeys with hand-drawn illustrations ranging from simple outlines to intricate patterns, accompanied by fascinating facts about our planet's flora, fauna, and cultures.

Take advantage of this artistic adventure that blends relaxation with education. "Colorful Journeys" is perfect as a personal treat or a thoughtful gift. Grab your copy today and transform any moment into an exploration of creativity and calm.
ISBN: 9798323334452